Fall Is Here!

Fall is here!

by Dorothy Sterling

illustrated by Winifred Lubell

published for The American Museum of Natural History by

THE NATURAL HISTORY PRESS / GARDEN CITY, NEW YORK

Books by Dorothy Sterling

BIOGRAPHY

CAPTAIN OF THE PLANTER,
  The Story of Robert Smalls
FREEDOM TRAIN,
  The Story of Harriet Tubman

LIFT EVERY VOICE: *The Lives of W. E. B. Dubois, Booker T. Washington, M. C. Terrell, and James W. Johnson* (written with Benjamin Quarles)
LUCRETIA MOTT, *Gentle Warrior*

FICTION

THE BROWNIE SCOUT MYSTERY
THE CUB SCOUT MYSTERY
* ELLEN'S BLUE JAYS

MARY JANE
THE SECRET OF THE OLD POST BOX
THE SILVER SPOON MYSTERY

NON-FICTION

* CATERPILLARS
* CREATURES OF THE NIGHT
* FALL IS HERE!
FOREVER FREE, *The Story of the Emancipation Proclamation*
INSECTS AND THE HOMES THEY BUILD
POLIO PIONEERS

* SPRING IS HERE!
* THE STORY OF CAVES
THE STORY OF MOSSES, FERNS, AND MUSHROOMS
TREES AND THEIR STORY
UNITED NATIONS, N. Y.
WALL STREET, *The Story of the Stock Exchange*

* Illustrated by Winifred Lubell

The National History Press, publisher for The American Museum of Natural History, is a division of Doubleday & Company, Inc. The Press is directed by an editorial board made up of members of the staff of both the Museum and Doubleday. The Natural History Press has its editorial offices at The American Museum of Natural History, Central Park West at 79th Street, New York, New York 10024, and its business offices at 501 Franklin Avenue, Garden City, New York.

Contents

1.   A Getting-Ready Time

Go outdoors some bright September morning and look and listen. All at once you know that today is different from the warm drowsy days of August. There's a feeling of excitement in the air. Something is happening.

The leaves are turning orange, yellow, and flaming red. Purple grapes hang from the vines. The pointed pod of a milkweed splits open and hundreds of seeds float away on the breeze.

A flock of noisy robins settles on the branches of a tree. A pair of ducks waddles along the shore. Suddenly the birds fly off, heading south.

A turtle inches across the road. A chipmunk darts into its burrow, its cheeks bulging with seeds. Crickets lay eggs. Squirrels bury acorns. A caterpillar swings from a branch, spinning a cocoon.

Summer is over. Fall is here!

The Speeding Earth

The story of fall starts with the sun and with the spinning, speeding earth we live on. All during the year the earth travels around the blazing sun. Day and night, month after month, the earth follows an oval path around the sun. The trip takes about 365 days to complete, but the earth doesn't stop then. It keeps on traveling around and around.

All during the year the fiery sun warms the earth. Its light gives trees and flowers the energy they need to grow. Animals feed on the plants. Larger animals eat the smaller ones. If it weren't for the sun, our earth would be a rocky wasteland. No trees or birds or people could live on it.

The sun shines steadily all year, but different parts of the earth get different amounts of sunshine at different times. That's because of the way the earth moves. As it speeds through space, it spins like a top that's tipped to one side. In winter, the northern part of the earth is tipped away from the sun. In summer, it leans toward it.

The sun shines straight down on the northern hemisphere in the summer. The farther north you go then, the more sunlight you see. At the North Pole the sun shines day and night for twenty-four hours. In Alaska the days are eighteen hours long. Places like San Francisco and New York have fifteen hours of sunshine.

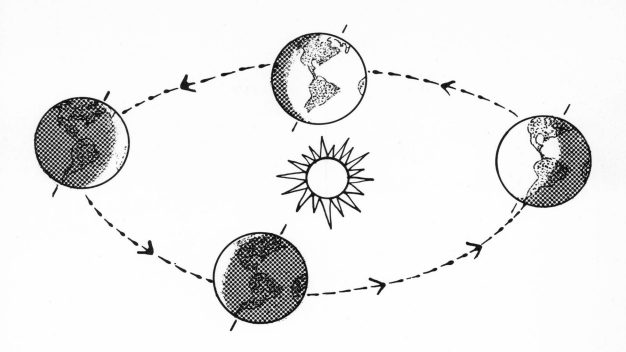

The farther south you go the less sunlight you see in the summer. Way down at the South Pole you won't see the sun at all. The cold gloomy night lasts for twenty-four hours. When it's summer in the northern hemisphere where we live, it's winter in Australia and South America.

As the earth moves on its endless path, the North Pole begins to tip away from the sun. The change comes slowly. But by the end of the summer, the sun doesn't shine for twenty-four hours at the North Pole. Instead, it is shining straight down on the equator, halfway between the two poles.

On September 22 (or sometimes on September 21 or 23) all the land above the equator and all the land below it gets the same amount of sunshine. Day and night are twelve hours long everywhere. September 22 is the first day of fall.

Still the earth speeds on. The North Pole leans farther and farther away from the sun. One day there's a minute less sunshine. Then two minutes. Three. Four. The minutes add up and become hours. By December people in San Francisco and New York see less than nine hours of sunlight each day. Even in Texas and Florida and southern California the sun shines for only ten hours.

There is less sunlight in the fall. There is also less heat because the sun's rays are slanting when they reach us. The air grows colder. The ground becomes colder. The water in lakes and ponds starts to freeze. Instead of summer thunder showers we have icy rain and snow.

For people in towns and cities, these changes scarcely matter. We say, "Bit of a nip in the air" or "Getting dark earlier these days." If it's cold, we turn on the heat. If it's dark, we turn on the lights. There's plenty of food in the grocery store even when snow covers the ground. And gas stations sell antifreeze so that the water in our car motors won't turn to ice.

But an oak tree can't flip a light switch. A robin can't go to the grocery store for worms. And have you ever seen a chipmunk turn on the heat, or a frog pour a can of antifreeze into a pond?

The earth has been circling the sun in its lopsided way for billions of years. During that long, long time, plants and animals have developed their own ways to meet the changing seasons. When the North Pole tips away from the sun, every living thing, from the tallest tree to the smallest flea, gets ready for winter—and next spring.

2.   The Trees' Way

During the long summer days the roots of the birch tree soak up water from the soil. Gallons and gallons of water travel up the trunk of the tree to its leaves. In the sunlight, the green leaves use some of this water from the soil, and carbon dioxide from the air around them, to make food. The rest of the water escapes into the air through tiny holes in the leaves.

All summer the food made in the birch leaves moves to different parts of the tree. The tree's roots and branches grow longer. Its trunk thickens. New green leaves unfold. Buds form. Seeds ripen.

What do you think would happen if the birch tree kept on growing this way during the fall and winter? One cold morning, the water in the soil would freeze. The tree wouldn't be able to soak up gallons of water any more. The water in the leaves would freeze too. As it expanded into ice, the ice would smash the food-making machinery in the leaves. The tree wouldn't be able to make any more food. Without food and water, the birch tree would die.

Fortunately, this doesn't happen. Because as the days become shorter and the nights colder, the birch tree slows down. No more new leaves unfold. No more buds form. Food from the leaves is stored in the trunk where it will be safe until next spring.

But the tree still must protect its thin delicate leaves. How can it prevent them from freezing? The answer is, it can't. Instead, it closes its food factories for the winter. It shuts up shop by shedding its leaves.

If all its leaves were to break off suddenly on the first cold day, the branches of the birch would be covered with tiny cuts. Water would ooze out of the cuts. Insects could creep in, along with germs that cause disease.

But this doesn't happen either. Because way back in August the birch tree gets ready to drop its leaves. Way back in August, a *separation layer* forms at the bottom of the stem of each leaf. After several weeks, this separation layer becomes dry and crumbly—so dry and so crumbly that the slightest puff of wind can blow the leaf away. Meanwhile a layer of cork forms too, just below the separation layer. When the leaf falls, the cork covers the cut on the branch. Instead of open wounds, there are scars showing where the leaves used to be.

Birch

Maple

The Painted Leaves of Fall

While these changes are taking place, every leaf on the birch turns yellow. The maples are flaming orange or red. The hickories are gold, the ash leaves are the color of ripe plums. The oaks turn scarlet, rose, bronze.

People used to say, "Jack Frost painted the autumn leaves." It wasn't a good explanation. It certainly wasn't accurate because the leaves turn before the first frosts come. The painted leaves of fall really start with those layers in the leaf stems.

Little by little, the "pipes" that connect the leaves and branches become stuffed up. Less water flows into the leaves. Less food travels away from them. By this time the leaves aren't making as much food because they have fewer hours of daylight in which to work.

Oak

Hickory

Ash

As the food factories in the leaves slow down, their green coloring matter—called *chlorophyll*—gradually disappears. It bleaches—in somewhat the way that a green sock turns white if there is too much bleach in the wash water. Only the leaves of fall don't turn white. That's because they contain other colors besides chlorophyll green. There are yellow and orange colors in the leaves. They have been in the leaves all summer, but they were hidden by the chlorophyll. After the green fades, you can see them.

15

This explains why birch leaves turn gold in the fall, but it doesn't explain the scarlet oak or the crimson maple or the deep purple of the ash. The reds and purples are brand-new. They don't show up in the leaves at all until summer is over. Scientists are still finding out how they form. In part it has to do with chemical changes that take place when the stuffed-up pipes keep food from moving from the leaves. In part it has to do with the soil in which a tree grows. Sunshine makes these colors brighter. So does a drop in temperature at night.

It's like baking a cake. You have to use the right kind of pan. You have to put in the right amounts of flour and sugar. Your oven has to be the right heat. When everything is exactly right, the cake is really good.

An Englishwoman visiting the United States in the fall said, "The whole country goes to glory!" She had never seen anything like our painted leaves. In England the leaves turn pale yellow and dull brown. They are seldom red. That's because fall days there are cloudy and fall nights warm.

In New England, on the other hand, fall days are sparkling and the nights are cool. Trees, soil, sunshine, everything is exactly right—and a rainbow of colors glows from the leaves. There is scarcely any place in the world that can match the crazy-quilt show of color that lights up the eastern half of the United States and neighboring Canada each fall.

Live Oak

Joshua Tree

Palm

Ever Green

If you live in the West or South perhaps you think this is boasting. But almost all the trees in the forests of the Northwest are firs or pines or hemlocks. Their leaves are narrow, with a tough waxy covering that protects them from winter weather. They don't shed their leaves in the fall. Their leaves are green throughout the year.

The live oaks and magnolias of the South, the palms that grow in Florida and California, and the scraggly Joshua trees of the desert stay green in winter too. Most of these trees live where the weather is warm. Their food factories work even in January.

Don't Burn the Blanket

For two weeks or three, the country "goes to glory." Then comes a gust of wind, a spatter of raindrops and the show is over. As you watch the leaves drift to the ground it's easy to understand why this time of the year used to be called the "fall of the leaf," a name that we have shortened to fall.

The bright colors of the leaves fade quickly. Soon the woods are covered with a blanket of brown. Have you ever wondered about this leaf blanket? As new leaves are added, year after year, why aren't there mountains of leaves piling up around the trees?

Even on the ground, the leaves still contain food. Earthworms, millipedes, and other creatures so tiny that you can't see them nibble on the leaves. Small plants—pale mushrooms and their relatives—feed on the leaves too. The leaves are chewed, softened, and digested until they are changed into *leaf mold*. Then the leaf mold is broken up into still finer bits. After another year or so it becomes rich, dark, spongy soil.

Sometime when you take a walk in the woods pick up a handful of soil. Squeeze it. Smell it. You'll notice right away that it's different from the soil in backyards and gardens. It holds water better. It contains more plant food.

If people were to tidy up the woods each fall, raking the leaves together and burning them, there would be no leaf mold. There would be no rich soil. After a while there would be no woods.

Of course, it's different when leaves fall near homes. No one wants a blanket of leaves on the sidewalk or on the lawn, where it will smother the grass. But even these leaves can be raked under bushes or spread out over a flower bed. There's no need to burn them.

Many towns don't allow leaf bonfires any more. Besides the danger of fires spreading, the smoke from the leaves adds to the smog in the air. In some cities, the leaves collected from the streets are dumped into deep pits. Later, leaf mold is dug from the pits and mixed with the soil in the parks.

Do you know what your town does with its blanket of leaves in the fall?

Beech

Horse Chestnut

A Surprise

After the leaves have fallen, the bare branches of the trees look dead. But they aren't dead. Or bare.

The first time you *really* look at a birch tree in the fall you're in for a surprise. Every branch is covered with pointed yellow and brown buds. Although these are called *winter buds,* they grew during the summer. You didn't notice them then because the leaves hid them.

If you pull back a bud's waterproof wrapping with a pin, you will be able to see what's inside. Leaves. Tiny, shiny, twisted, folded leaves.

The buds stay on the tree all winter. In the spring when water travels up the trunk again, their outer coverings drop off. Then the crumpled leaves unfold, grow bigger, turn green.

At the end of some birch branches there is another larger bud, stuffed with yellow-green flowers. The flowers are hard to see even with a magnifying glass but they will open too when spring comes.

Each kind of tree makes its own kind of winter bud. There are long, needle-sharp buds on the beech and the cottonwood. There are stubby, woolly buds on the apple and fat, gold-colored ones on the hickory. The sticky

Apple

20

Cottonwood

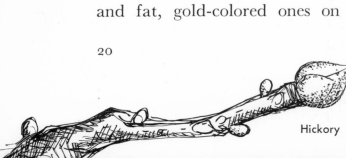

Hickory

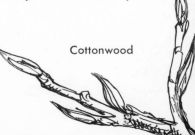

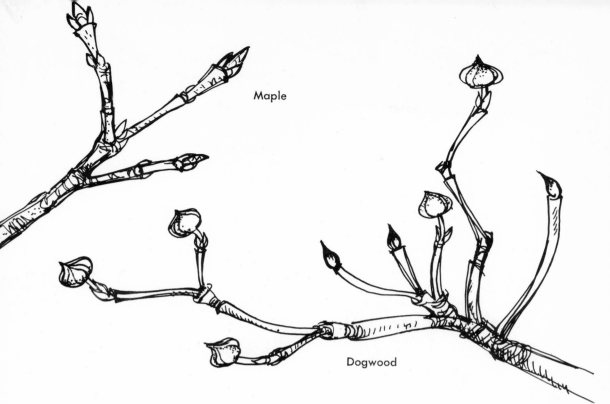

Maple

Dogwood

horse chestnut buds feel as if they had been varnished.

Oak buds are oval. They grow in an untidy cluster at the tip of a twig and along the sides of the branch. The shiny maple buds are neatly spaced. At the branch tips they grow in threes, with a large bud in the middle and a smaller one on either side. You can always recognize a maple in the fall by these bud triplets.

On most trees, leaf and flower buds are shaped alike, although the flower buds are often larger. The dogwood, like the birch, has two styles of buds—a pointed red one which contains leaves and a round gray one for its flowers. Some freezing day when spring seems far away try counting the fat gray buds on a dogwood. You will be able to tell your friends that in six months the tree will have 78—or 99—or 137 flowers. They'll think that you're a fortune-teller!

Oak

Birch

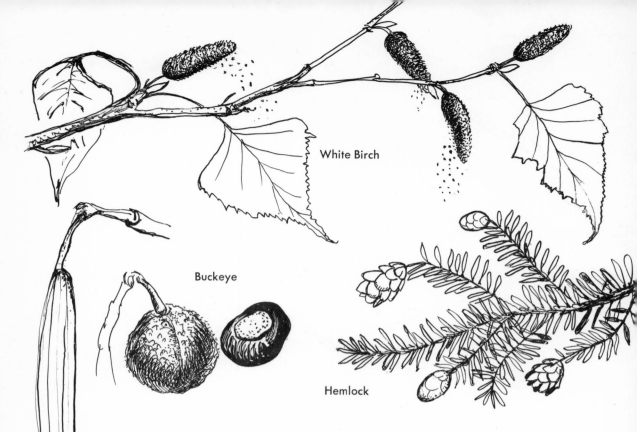

White Birch

Buckeye

Hemlock

Have some Fruit

There's something else on the branches of the birch. It looks like a little pine cone, but be careful how you handle it. At the slightest touch it will fall apart and dozens of papery seeds will drop to the ground.

This is the fruit of the birch tree. Probably you think of fruit as something good to eat. When botanists, the scientists who study plants, talk of fruit they mean a plant's seeds and the container in which the seeds grow.

Apples and oranges are fruits. But so are acorns and hickory nuts and the shiny buckeyes that boys like to carry in their pockets. And the red berries on holly trees. And the round balls on sycamores. And the long pods that dangle from catalpa and mesquite branches. And

Catalpa

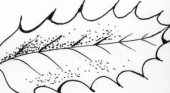

Holly

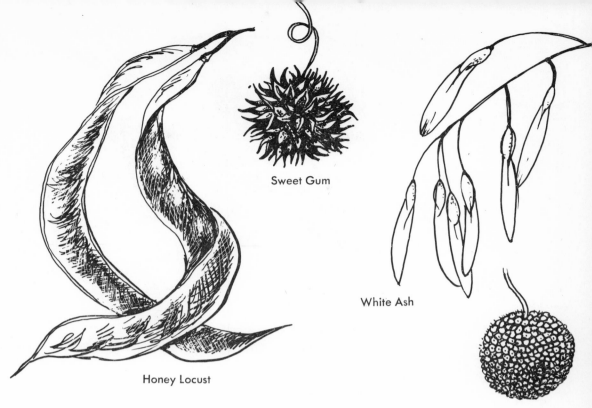

Sweet Gum

White Ash

Honey Locust

Sycamore

the thimble-sized cones of the hemlock and the foot-long cones of the sugar pine.

You will see many different kinds of the tree fruits in the fall. There are clumps of paddle-shaped seeds on the ash tree. Each seed has a papery wing so that it can sail through the air. The big pods on honey locusts remind you of overripe bananas when they turn brown. Their twisted shape helps them to skate across the icy ground. The seeds inside these locust pods have a sweet taste. Some people like to suck them.

The prickly woody fruits of sweet gum trees sway back and forth, spilling out seeds. The seed balls of the sycamore hang from the tree all winter. Snow and ice coat them with frosting until they look like little cup-cakes.

23

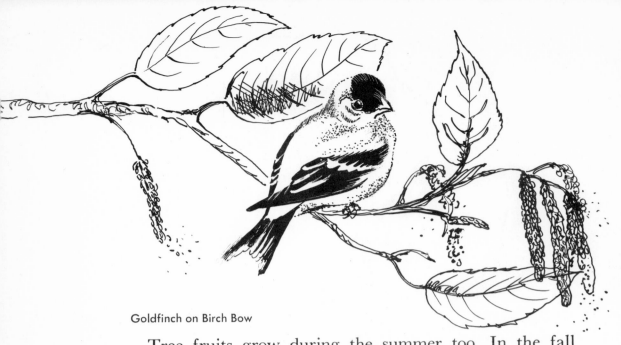

Goldfinch on Birch Bow

Tree fruits grow during the summer too. In the fall when the seeds are ripe it's time to harvest them. Birds help with the harvest. They eat the red berries on the dogwood and madrone. But the seeds inside the berries are too hard to digest. As the birds fly through the woods they drop them. Cardinals and finches eat birch seeds. And each time they peck at the dry birch fruit, they scatter seeds to the winds.

Squirrels plant the seeds. They bury acorns and nuts and pine seeds—and apples if they can find them. After

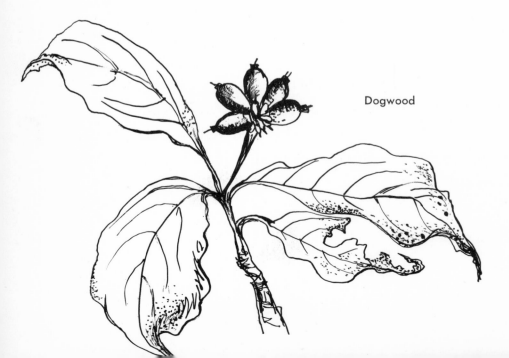

Dogwood

a while the shell of the buried nut splits. The flesh of the apple rots. The seeds inside start to grow.

Most tree seeds rest during the cold months, but a few sprout in the fall. If you scuffle through the leaves under an oak in November, you can probably find an acorn. Its cap has fallen off and two white shoots are poking through its shell. One will form the roots of an oak tree, the other its trunk and leaves.

But which is which? You can find out by burying the sprouting seed. Try planting it sideways. Try turning it around and around. No matter what you do, and no matter how many times you do it, the shoot that is going to be the trunk will always grow upward, while the root shoot grows down.

Gray Squirrel

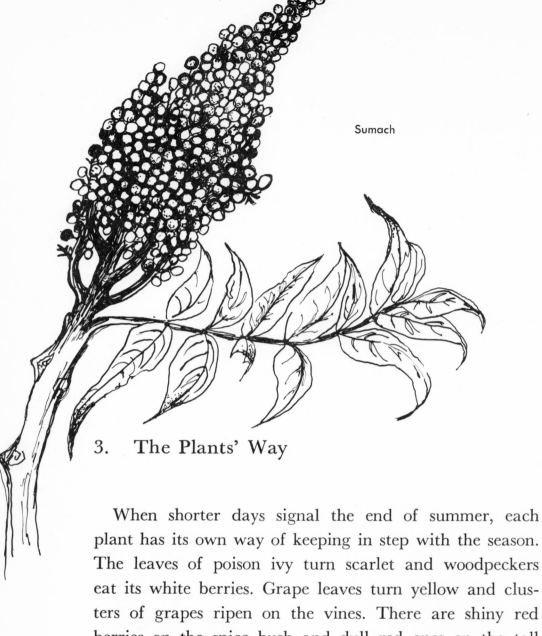

Sumach

3.   The Plants' Way

When shorter days signal the end of summer, each plant has its own way of keeping in step with the season. The leaves of poison ivy turn scarlet and woodpeckers eat its white berries. Grape leaves turn yellow and clusters of grapes ripen on the vines. There are shiny red berries on the spice bush and dull red ones on the tall spires of the sumac.

All these vines and bushes shed their leaves in the fall. Like the trees, they have buds on their branches and food stored in their woody stems. When spring comes they will grow again.

26

Poison Ivy

A few bushes are evergreen. The rhododendrons that people often plant near their homes have a special trick for cold weather. Their broad leathery leaves curl inward when the temperature drops. The colder the day the tighter the curl of the leaves. At 20 degrees they droop from the branches like wet wash on a line. As soon as the temperature rises, they uncurl again. If you want to know how cold it is outdoors, look at a rhododendron instead of a thermometer!

Rhododendron Leaves
in Warm and Freezing Weather

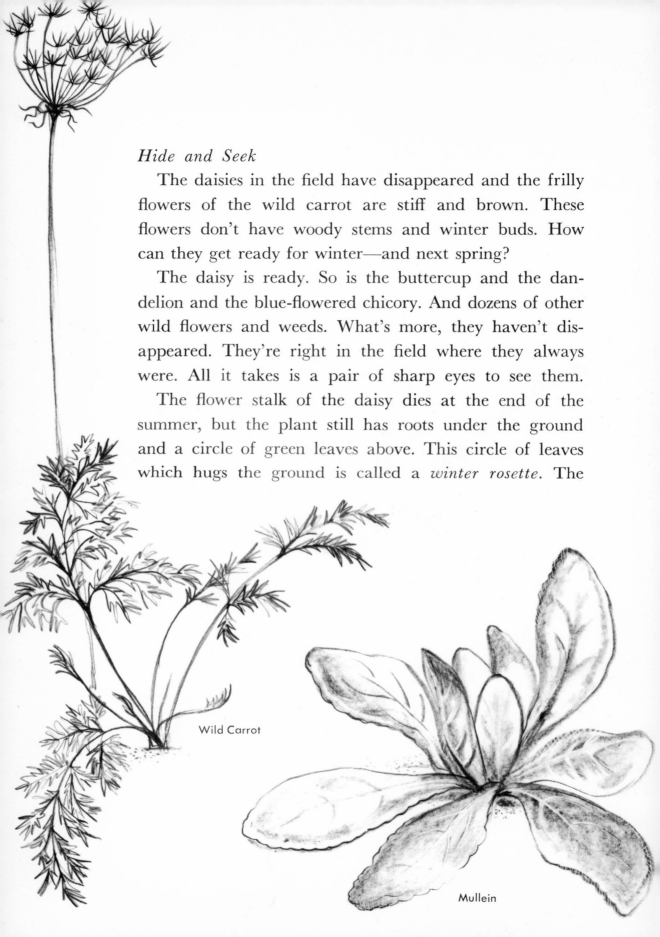

Hide and Seek

The daisies in the field have disappeared and the frilly flowers of the wild carrot are stiff and brown. These flowers don't have woody stems and winter buds. How can they get ready for winter—and next spring?

The daisy is ready. So is the buttercup and the dandelion and the blue-flowered chicory. And dozens of other wild flowers and weeds. What's more, they haven't disappeared. They're right in the field where they always were. All it takes is a pair of sharp eyes to see them.

The flower stalk of the daisy dies at the end of the summer, but the plant still has roots under the ground and a circle of green leaves above. This circle of leaves which hugs the ground is called a *winter rosette*. The

Wild Carrot

Mullein

leaves stay green even when it snows. They hold the daisy's place in the field, marking time until spring.

Once you have spotted the daisy's, you'll find other winter rosettes. Each kind is different, of course. The wild carrot's leaves are feathery, just as they are in summer, and the big broad leaves of the mullein are velvet-smooth.

Not all flowers form winter rosettes. No matter how carefully you look you won't find the leaves of daffodils or Jack-in-the-pulpits in fall. But they haven't disappeared either. Along with violets and lilies—and carrots and potatoes and onions—they hide under the ground. They store away food in roots or special thick stems.

Taking apart an onion will give you an idea of how some of these underground storehouses work. Its layers of scales are packed with food. When you peel off the scales—and wipe away your tears—you will find a pointed white bud in the center. Inside this bud are leaves, all ready to grow when the weather turns warm.

Some plants really do disappear in the fall. The giant ragweed and the little cocklebur, the tall wild lettuce and the clinging morning glory vine—these and a host of garden flowers live for only a few months. After a frost, their leaves turn brown, their stalks wither and their roots die.

But this doesn't mean that there won't be any ragweed next summer. Or any flowers in the garden. Before they disappear, the weeds and flowers make seeds.

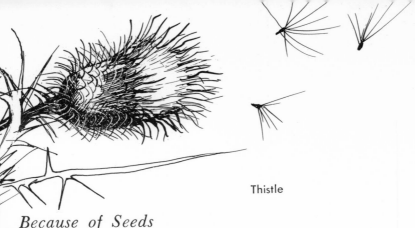

Thistle

Because of Seeds

Tall trees can topple in winter storms. Flat leaf rosettes and fat underground stems can be uprooted. But even if every leaf and bud and root were killed, the earth would still turn green in the spring.

Because of seeds.

The plump pod of the milkweed opens as it dries. Inside are hundreds of neatly-packed seeds.

The sunflower no longer faces the sun. Its once-yellow head flops over, heavy with seeds.

The cattail in the swamp seems hard, but if you poke it with your finger, the spike bursts. Like a torn pillow, it spills out fluff—and seeds.

The ragged thistle is a cloud of silk—and seeds. There are seeds in the purple grape and the orange pumpkin. There are seeds in the prickly balls of the burdock. Have you been walking outdoors? Then there are probably seeds all over your jacket.

Every seed has the beginnings of a plant inside it. Every seed has food for its plant to grow on, and a hard outer coat that protects the plant from dryness and from cold. The brown seeds in the milkweed pod will grow into milkweed plants. The tiny dots in the cattail fluff are the tiny beginnings of the cattails' tall spikes.

30

Sunflower

You can see these beginnings for yourself in a sun-flower seed. (If sunflowers don't grow in your neighbor-hood, you can buy their seeds in the supermarket. They are sold for wild bird food.) Try cracking one of these striped seeds the way a squirrel does—with your teeth. Inside you will see the tip of the sunflower-to-be and the food that's wrapped around it. You can eat the food, too. It has a sweet nutty taste.

Do you notice how tough the striped seed coat is? A sunflower seed can be frozen in an ice cube without killing the plant inside. But what do you think would happen if you baked some of the seeds in an oven? Can their winter coats protect them from too much heat?

31

See the World

For most of their lives weeds and flowers are stay-at-homes. They dig their roots into the ground, hold their leaves to the light, and that's all. During a few weeks in the fall they go traveling.

Sometimes the whole plant leaves home. When their seeds are ripe and their stems dry, tumbleweeds break away from their roots. They roll across the ground, slowly on a calm day, faster and faster if the wind is blowing. Wherever they wander, the rolling tumbleweeds scatter seeds.

A botanist once found more than 180,000 shiny black seeds on a single tumbleweed plant. If all these seeds were to fall close to the parent plant, they would crowd each other out. By leaving home in the fall, a tumbleweed gives its seeds a better start in life.

Several different kinds of plants have the tumbleweed habit. The Russian thistle is one of the most successful—or the peskiest, depending on whether you take the weed's or the farmer's viewpoint. You have probably seen pictures of it in cowboy films. Twice as big as a basketball,

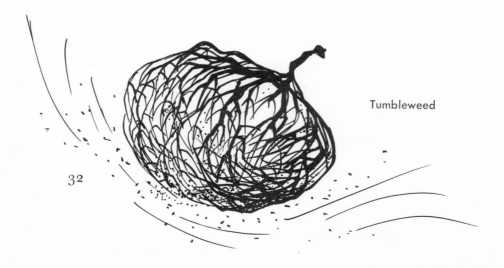

Tumbleweed

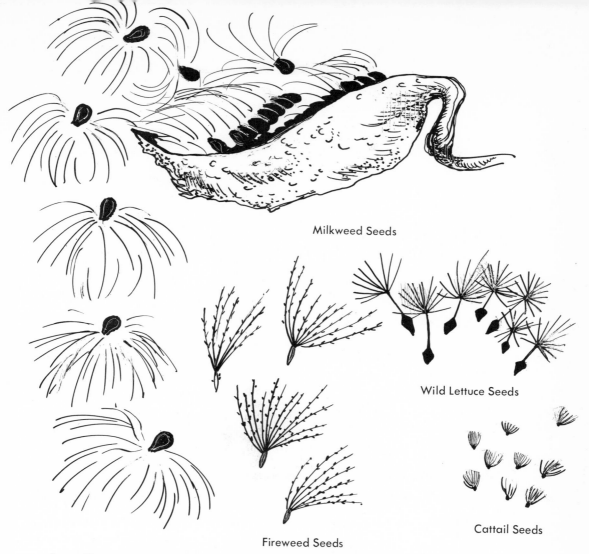

Milkweed Seeds

Wild Lettuce Seeds

Cattail Seeds

Fireweed Seeds

it rolls across the western plains, planting its seeds from Canada to Mexico.

Milkweeds—and cattails and wild lettuce and tall purple fireweed—have found another way to travel. With silky tufts acting as parachutes, their seeds float on the breeze. If you bring a milkweed pod (which is really the fruit of the milkweed) indoors, you will find that the currents of air in the room are enough to start the seeds flying. Outdoors they can travel two or three miles from their parent plant.

Sticktights

Burdock

Many seeds hitch a ride in the fall. You don't even have to look for the hitchhikers. Just walk through the weeds and they'll find you. As you pull off the burrs and sticktights, you will see that all of them have curved hooks. These hooks catch in an animal's fur. Wherever the animal goes, the seeds go too.

Years ago, pioneers crossing the prairies were surprised to see circles of weeds. Surely no one had planted these circles. What made the weeds grow that way?

The answer was buffaloes. Buffaloes whose fur was long and thick in the fall when seeds were ripening. During the day herds of these huge beasts grazed on the prairie. At night they formed a circle, putting their calves in the center where they would be safe. Settling down to sleep or stretching their legs in the morning, the buffaloes shook their manes—and shook out seeds.

34

Tick Trefoil

Cockleburrs

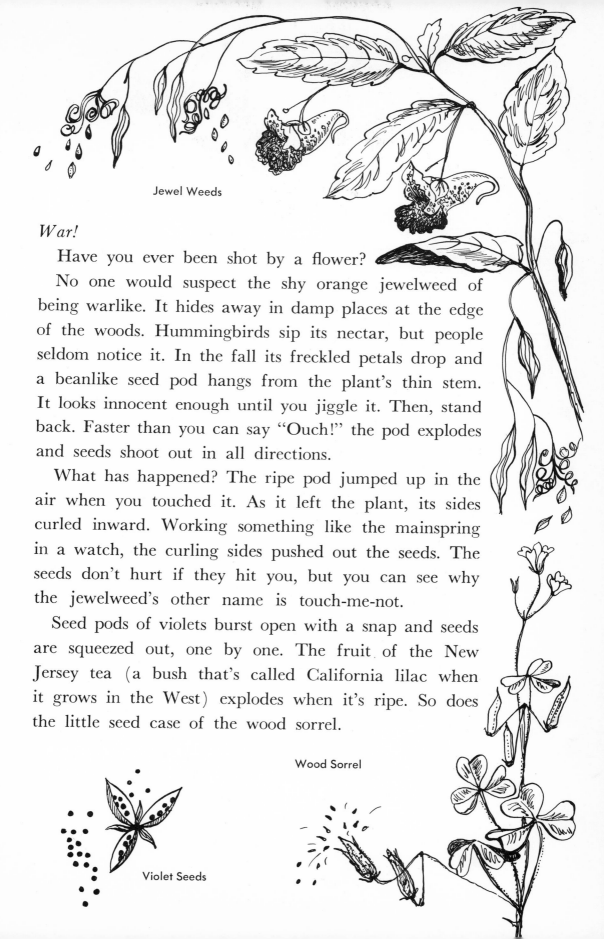

Jewel Weeds

War!

Have you ever been shot by a flower?

No one would suspect the shy orange jewelweed of being warlike. It hides away in damp places at the edge of the woods. Hummingbirds sip its nectar, but people seldom notice it. In the fall its freckled petals drop and a beanlike seed pod hangs from the plant's thin stem. It looks innocent enough until you jiggle it. Then, stand back. Faster than you can say "Ouch!" the pod explodes and seeds shoot out in all directions.

What has happened? The ripe pod jumped up in the air when you touched it. As it left the plant, its sides curled inward. Working something like the mainspring in a watch, the curling sides pushed out the seeds. The seeds don't hurt if they hit you, but you can see why the jewelweed's other name is touch-me-not.

Seed pods of violets burst open with a snap and seeds are squeezed out, one by one. The fruit of the New Jersey tea (a bush that's called California lilac when it grows in the West) explodes when it's ripe. So does the little seed case of the wood sorrel.

Wood Sorrel

Violet Seeds

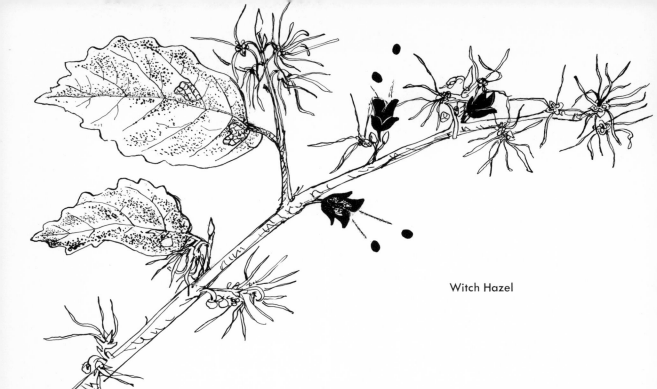

Witch Hazel

But for a really big gun nothing beats a witch hazel. Late in the fall, the brown fruits on its branches act like cannons. Double-barreled cannons with breeches loaded. When the cannons are good and dry, they fire. Shiny black seeds whizz past—left, right, center—until you feel as if you were caught in a bombardment.

Before you surrender to the enemy, look at the witch hazel branches again. Close to the cannon-like fruit there are flowers. Yes, flowers.

The Flowers of Fall

Wherever you go in fall you see bright leaves and withered stems and faded flowers. Except for the bright flowers on the witch hazel. And the yellow goldenrod and purple asters by the side of the road. And the blue gentians in the meadow and chrysanthemums in the garden.

36

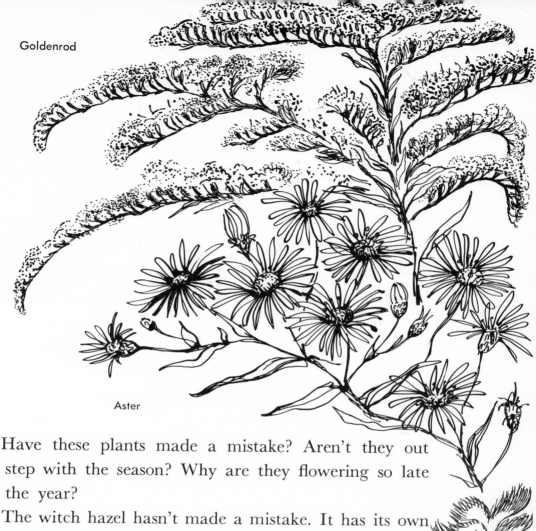

Goldenrod

Aster

Have these plants made a mistake? Aren't they out of step with the season? Why are they flowering so late in the year?

The witch hazel hasn't made a mistake. It has its own way of getting ready for winter. When its flower petals fall, its fruits take twelve months to ripen. The cannonballs that shoot from the stubby guns of the witch hazel have been growing and ripening for a whole year.

The goldenrod and asters and gentians aren't out of step either. They always flower in the fall, just as daffodils flower in the spring and daisies in the summertime.

But to say that something *always* happens doesn't explain the reason for it. Why doesn't goldenrod bloom in the spring? Why aren't there asters in the summer? Why should there be fall flowers anyway?

Fringed Gentian

Solving a Puzzle

About fifty years ago two botanists found some of the answers to these questions. They were puzzled by a tobacco plant that grew like Jack's beanstalk. At the end of the summer the tobacco was fifteen feet tall, with big broad leaves. But it didn't flower or produce seeds.

The botanists tried all sorts of different experiments. They gave the plants good soil, poor soil, lots of water, no water. No matter what they tried, they couldn't get the tobacco to flower. Then they started some of the tobacco in a greenhouse in the fall. To their surprise, it bloomed when it was three feet tall.

The tobacco hadn't flowered during the long summer days. Instead, it bloomed in the fall as the days grew short. Could it be—could it possibly be the shorter days that made the difference?

Until that time people had taken it for granted that the more hours of light a plant received the better off it

Mammoth Tobacco Blooming

would be. The botanists found that this wasn't true. After experimenting with different plants they discovered that some are *long-day plants*. They bloom in the summer when the days are long. Others, like the puzzling tobacco, are *short-day plants*. Their flowers open only in the spring or fall. Still other plants bloom in any season, as long as it isn't too hot or cold for them.

Daisies and black-eyed Susans and wild carrot are long-day plants. They flower when the summer sun is high in the sky. Goldenrod and asters grow right near them during the summer, but they don't flower until the North Pole tips away from the sun. They *can't* flower until they have twelve or thirteen hours of sunlight. The blue gentians and the yellow witch hazel must wait even longer. Their flowers don't open until the sun shines for eleven hours, or less, each day.

The botanists called their discovery *photoperiodism*. (*Photo* comes from a Greek word meaning "light" and *period* is a division of time.) Photoperiodism explained why goldenrod and asters are as much a part of fall as flaming maple leaves or orange pumpkins. Even more important, it gave people a whole new way of studying the different seasons. Since its discovery, scientists have been investigating the effect of short and long days on the lives of squirrels and fish, birds and bats and butterflies. They now think that animals as well as plants are influenced by the changing hours of daylight as the earth speeds around the sun.

Tree Swallows

4.   The Birds' Way

Suddenly there's a burst of noise. Chirping robins cover the branches of the apple tree. Rows of swallows line up on the telephone wires. Ducks land on the pond. Blackbirds gather on the cattails in the swamp. Wherever you look there are chattering, cheeping, restless, hungry birds.

In a few days they are gone. The woods and fields are quiet. Only the wind sways the cattails in the swamp. Only a sparrow perches on the telephone wires. The birds have flown away.

Where do they go? Will they ever come back again?

Long ago the girls and boys of ancient Greece asked these same questions when the birds disappeared in the fall. Standing along the shore of the Mediterranean Sea, they could watch cranes flying south. They knew that these big long-legged birds spent the winter in Egypt, because travelers had seen them there. But it was hard to believe that a swallow or a lark could fly across the sea.

Some people thought that the smaller birds hopped onto the outstretched wings of the cranes and rode piggy-back to Africa. Others were sure that the little birds stayed in Greece and went into hiding. Swallows stripped themselves of their feathers and crawled into holes in the ground to sleep through the cold months, they said.

The story of the sleeping swallows grew bigger and better as the centuries passed. There were reports of featherless swallows on mountain tops, of swallows that buried themselves in the mud or dived to the bottom of a stream for a long winter's nap. In a book published in the sixteenth century a Swedish naturalist said that fishermen caught swallows in their nets in winter. "They cling beak to beak, wing to wing, foot to foot, having bound themselves together in the first days of autumn," he wrote. He even printed a drawing of a fisherman with a catch of fish and birds!

Here and there, scientists began to doubt these tales. In the eighteenth century a naturalist put some birds in an icebox. Instead of sleeping, they soon died. Another proved that it was impossible for birds to survive under water. Still other scientists visited warmer countries in the winter and saw swallows there.

Now we know that swallows—and robins and blackbirds and long-necked geese and broad-shouldered hawks and little brown wrens—*migrate* in the fall. To migrate means to travel regularly from one place to another. Unlike the traveling tumbleweed, the birds don't go wherever the wind carries them. They follow regular paths to their winter homes. They travel to the same places every year. And they do come back again.

Getting Ready

In the spring, the birds fly north. They spread out all over the United States and Canada. They build nests, lay eggs, and raise babies. The farther north they go, the more hours of daylight they have in which to work. Robins in Ohio spend sixteen hours a day bringing worms and insects to their nests. Robins in Alaska have twenty-one hours of daylight to hunt for food. Their babies grow up quickly.

In the summer the young birds leave their nests. They catch their own insects. They eat the fruit and seeds that are ripening. They have plenty to eat then, but their feast can't last forever. Soon most of the insects will die and the seeds will be covered with snow. All over the North, food will be hard to find. Long before that happens, the birds head for their winter homes.

They don't pack up and go on the first fall day. While the trees get ready to shed their leaves, the birds prepare

Geese Migrating

for their long trip. Perhaps you have found feathers on the ground at the end of summer. That's because the birds are *molting*. They lose their old worn feathers, one or two at a time, and new ones grow in. Underneath the feathers that you can see there are hundreds more—soft, downy ones next to their skins. Like the winter underwear that skiers wear, these feathers help to keep the birds warm.

Other changes take place inside the birds' bodies. Most of the food that they eat is stored as fat. This is a special *migration fat* which gives them energy for their flight. Even the birds' behavior changes.

You know how restless children are when school is almost over. Boys wriggle in their seats. Girls drum on their desks with their fingers or look up at the clock. Then, at last, the bell rings. Everyone picks up books and pencils and rushes to the door.

Birds act almost the same way in the fall. They're restless. They flit from branch to branch. They fly short distances from home and come back again. Then at last they crowd together. As if they had heard a bell ring, they all take off.

Where Do They Go?

If birds were businessmen you might read an advertisement like this some morning:

ENJOY SUMMER in the WINTERTIME
HOP ON THE ROBIN EXPRESS
FOLLOW THE SWALLOW LINE
THOUSANDS OF FLIGHTS EACH WEEK

Fares as low as
24 worms, 12 beetles, 47 seeds

FLY NOW, EAT LATER

The migrating birds go to many different places. The Robin Express has a short run. It drops off passengers in the southern United States. Its last stop is Florida. Blackbirds travel to Louisiana, Texas, and California. Tiny ruby-throated hummingbirds cross the Gulf of Mexico on their way to Panama. Warblers fly to the islands of the West Indies. Orioles go to Mexico, scarlet tanagers to Peru.

If you follow the Swallow Line, be prepared for a long trip with lots of stopovers. Swallows that nest in barns in Alaska fly to South America for the winter. Many stay in Brazil, but others travel on to Argentina, seven thousand miles from their summer home.

Golden plovers also spend the winter in Argentina. In the fall thousands of plovers (the word rhymes with "lovers") flock to Canada's east coast. After fattening up on insects and berries they take off across the open ocean. They fly day and night without stopping until they reach South America. Pacific golden plovers travel nonstop from Alaska to Hawaii, a distance of two thousand miles. Their trip wouldn't set a record for a jet plane, but remember that each of these feathered flying machines weighs less than a baseball.

Golden Plovers Migrating

Arctic Terns

Of all of the migrating birds, Arctic terns fly the farthest. They raise their babies within a few hundred miles of the North Pole. During their stay in the North, they have twenty-four hours of daylight most of the time. Before the long Arctic winter begins, they fly to the Antarctic—where they have twenty-four hours of daylight most of the time. Arctic terns see more of the sun each year than any other animal on earth!

46

Paths across the Sky

You have probably heard the saying, "Birds of a feather flock together." They don't, in the spring and summer. They pair off then, two by two, and chase other birds away from their nests. Only when they get ready to migrate do they become sociable. Then dozens of robins, hundreds of warblers, thousands of blackbirds flock together.

It's hard to picture the enormous number of birds that fly over the United States each fall. Sometimes you can see them when they drop down to rest. Sometimes you can hear them calling to each other as they fly by at night. They travel south along four great highways. Not paved roads, of course, but highways in the sky. Scientists call them *flyways*.

Almost all the birds who nest in the East follow the Atlantic Flyway which runs from New England to Florida. On narrow necks of land, places like Cape Cod in Massachusetts and Cape May in New Jersey, more than a hundred different kinds of birds—swallows and bluebirds, thrushes, kingbirds, cuckoos, warblers—can be seen at one time.

Another famous place for fall bird-watching is Hawk Mountain in Pennsylvania. On windy September days the big birds of prey—hawks, eagles, ospreys—glide by, so close to the top of the mountain that people standing there can almost touch them.

Swans, Ducks, and Canada Goose

Geese and ducks and graceful swans gather on the bays. You can see them on Jamaica Bay in New York, Delaware Bay, Chesapeake Bay, Back Bay in Virginia. Some stay for the winter. Others go on to the Carolinas and Florida.

In the West, birds follow the Pacific Flyway, between the Rockies and the Pacific Ocean. Or the Central Flyway that leads from Montana across the Great Plains to Texas. Sometimes there are a million ducks feeding in the marshes near the Bear River in Utah, or along the Klamath in

48

Oregon. The sky above California's Sacramento Valley grows dark as hundreds of thousands of blackbirds swoop down to roost.

The busiest of all the bird highways is the Mississippi Flyway, which runs from the Great Lakes to the Gulf of Mexico. Nighthawks and warblers, armies of sparrows and clouds of swallows fly along the shores of the Mississippi River. There are reasons why this flyway is so popular. Birds can travel along it for three thousand miles without meeting up with a mountain or even a hill of any size. They can find fish in the river, insects along its banks, and fruit in the nearby woods and fields. Like sensible tourists anywhere, they prefer a level road with plenty of nice places to stop along the way.

Don't Shoot the Whooping Crane!

Billions of birds take to the air in the fall, but countless thousands never reach their winter homes. Some are blown out to sea, or die in storms. Others crash into tall buildings and television towers. Until recently, however, the birds' worst danger has come from men—men with guns.

Perhaps you have heard of the passenger pigeon. When the Pilgrims landed at Plymouth these birds flew through the woods in fantastic numbers. The beating of their wings sounded like thunder. At night when they roosted, branches snapped under their weight and tree trunks bent to the ground.

Whooping Cranes

A naturalist tried to count a flock of passenger pigeons when they were migrating. He started early in the morning and at sunset he was still counting. The flock was a mile wide and 240 miles long, he figured. That's farther than from New York to Washington, or Chicago to Detroit!

The tremendous number of birds was an invitation to hunters—and almost everyone was a hunter in those days. Men shot and clubbed and trapped passenger pigeons. They broiled them, roasted them, pickled them, smoked them, and fed them to their hogs.

A hundred years ago, the passenger pigeons had been wiped out in the East, but they were still darkening the

50

western skies. As railroads crossed the continent, hunters followed the migrating flocks, slaughtering the birds and shipping carloads of them to city markets.

One fall a pigeon dealer announced that he had no more birds to sell. They had all flown to Australia, he said. They hadn't, of course. They were dead. The last passenger pigeon in the United States is a stuffed bird named Martha who roosts in a museum in Washington. The sign beside her says EXTINCT.

Today the best-known travelers on the flyways are the whooping cranes. Each fall when they fly from their nesting grounds in Canada to their winter home in Texas, their pictures are shown on television and radio announcers broadcast an appeal, "Don't shoot the whoopers!"

Once these tall majestic birds nested all over the Great Plains and spent winters in the East as well as the Southwest. Their migrating flocks were one of the great sights of fall. Their bugle-like call could be heard for miles. Then settlers cut down the forests and drained the swamps and shot the cranes. They blasted away at them until there were only fifteen or so whoopers left in the world.

At last groups of bird lovers stepped in. Scientists migrated north with the birds in the spring, and south in the fall to protect them. Their winter home was made a wildlife refuge. Naturalists hover over their nests in helicopters, counting eggs and babies and dropping down to rescue injured birds. Last year forty-four long-legged cranes traveled south along the Mississippi Flyway. There is hope that their flock will continue to grow.

In the years between the destruction of the passenger pigeons and the attempt to save the whoopers, people came to realize that EXTINCT is a very final sort of word. It means gone forever. Nothing that anybody can do will ever bring an extinct animal back to life again.

After many debates Congress passed laws to protect migrating birds. Treaties were signed with Canada and Mexico too, so that the birds would be safe when they crossed our borders. Hunters are no longer allowed to shoot birds as they fly south in the fall. A limited amount of hunting of ducks and geese is permitted, but only for a few weeks each year.

As important as the laws has been the purchase of woods and swamps, lakes and beaches where the migrating flocks can feed and roost. There are wildlife refuges along all the flyways now, close to three hundred of them at the last count.

It's too late for the passenger pigeons, but the story of the whoopers may have a happy ending after all.

Snow Bunting

Snow Birds

While robins and swallows fly away, chickadees and juncos arrive. Some birds don't migrate at all. Others travel short distances, from mountains to valleys, or from Canada to the northern part of the United States.

Contrary to what you may think, birds can stand a great deal of cold. Their bodies are about five degrees warmer than yours and their hearts beat much faster—fantastically fast on cold days. Their main problem in winter isn't zero weather—it's food.

Swallows, who feed on flying insects, have to go south in the fall. So do hummingbirds, who sip nectar from flowers. But some other birds are able to change their diets. Snow buntings, for instance, catch bugs in the summer, and eat seeds in the wintertime.

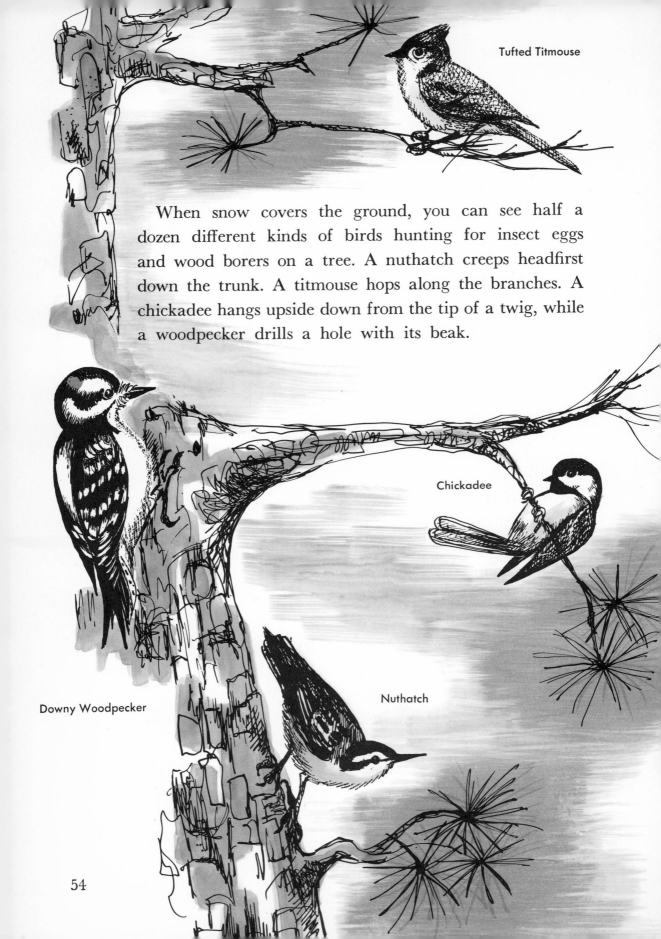

Tufted Titmouse

When snow covers the ground, you can see half a dozen different kinds of birds hunting for insect eggs and wood borers on a tree. A nuthatch creeps headfirst down the trunk. A titmouse hops along the branches. A chickadee hangs upside down from the tip of a twig, while a woodpecker drills a hole with its beak.

Chickadee

Nuthatch

Downy Woodpecker

Underneath the trees juncos and sparrows and cardinals scratch away the snow with their feet. Or they wriggle around, melting it with their warm bodies until they uncover seeds.

All of these birds are tamer in the fall. When food is scarce they call at people's homes, waiting for handouts. Do you notice how fat they are on cold days? That's because they fluff out their feathers. This gives them extra protection from the cold.

Cardinal

Song Sparrow

Junco

Fall and Winter Molt of Ptarmigans

The birds who don't migrate have another problem in the fall and winter. When the trees are bare and frosts have cut down the tall weeds, the big chicken-like birds who roost on the ground can't hide as they did in summer. They are right out in the open where owls and foxes can pounce on them.

Ptarmigans (the *p* isn't pronounced), who stay in the Far North, change color when they molt. They lose their brown feathers and grow white ones. They match the snow so perfectly that it's hard for enemies to spot them.

The ptarmigans also grow rows of scaly bristles on their toes. These bristles are a combination of snowshoe and shovel. They help the bird to walk on the snow without sinking in, and to tunnel under it at night.

In our northern woods, ruffed grouse and bobwhites

56

take shelter under the snow too. At night a bobwhite family huddles together. They sleep in a circle, arranging themselves like the spokes of a wheel, with tails touching and heads pointing outward. If danger threatens, they all take off at once, flying in different directions.

Bobwhites

Have you ever watched a male pheasant in the fall? His bronze and gold feathers are almost the same color as the fallen leaves. He strolls slowly through the woods as if he knew that he was invisible. When he walks across a lawn where his feathers don't match the ground cover, he runs, scooting across the grass like a scared chicken.

Keeping Track of the Birds

Even an expert bird-watcher has trouble telling one robin or sparrow from any other robin or sparrow. Birds don't have fingerprints or birthmarks. How can we tell them apart? How can we be sure that the birds who spend summers in our yards are the same birds that fly to Florida and Argentina? Or that the birds that arrive in the fall have come from Canada?

We can't—unless they are marked. Unless they have little tags on their legs.

The idea of tying messages to birds' legs is an old one. People used to do it for fun. It was like tossing a bottle into the ocean with a note inside. They hoped that someone would find their message and answer it, but most of the time no one did.

About seventy years ago a Danish schoolteacher became interested in tracking birds. He made up some little metal bands with his name, address, and a number on them. Fall after fall, he caught migrating birds. He fastened his bands to their legs and then set them free.

After a while he began to get letters from different countries. When his bands were returned he could tell from the numbers which birds had been found. He could say positively that a stork he had tagged in Denmark had flown to France or Italy. He wasn't just guessing. He *knew* where the stork had gone.

Banding birds caught on quickly after that. Today there are networks of bird-banders on every continent.

In North America the U. S. Fish and Wildlife Service works with the Canadian Wildlife Service to keep records of all the birds that have been banded—more than eleven million in the last fifty years.

Teams of volunteers help the two governments to do the banding. Sometimes they tag young birds before they leave their nests. More often they trap flocks of migrating birds in fine mesh nets. Handling the birds carefully so as not to hurt them, they fasten lightweight aluminum tags to their legs. They have tiny bands for hummingbirds, big broad ones for geese and swans and special tags that fit on the flippers of penguins. Like a dog's license or the identity bracelets that people often wear, these numbered bands will identify the birds no matter where they go.

Bird-banders must be at least eighteen years old, but

everyone can be on the lookout for marked birds. If you find one, write to the Bird Banding Office in Laurel, Maryland. Copy the numbers on the band and tell where and when you found it. If the bird is dead, flatten out the band and send it with your letter. If the bird is alive, let it go. You might see it again sometime.

In a few weeks you will hear from the Bird Banding Office. They will tell you what kind of bird you found and the date and place where it was banded. Then you will *know* where the bird came from.

Scientists have other ways of tracking migrating birds. One of the newest is *radar*. Radar was used during World War II to spot the approach of enemy airplanes. Early in the war, watchers on the coast of England saw bright dots on their radar screens (which are a little like television screens). They knew that the larger dots were planes, but they couldn't agree on the smaller ones. They called these mysterious dots "angels."

As radar was improved at the end of the war, more and more angels were seen. Most radar experts thought that the dots were caused by changes in the weather, but some men disagreed. After watching a procession of angels move across a radar screen, a Swiss scientist took out after them in a small plane. Just as he had suspected, the angels were birds!

Because songbirds usually fly at night when they are migrating, no one had been able to follow their trips until radar came along. An angel-watcher can't see every bird in the sky, but he can get a good idea of the size of the

Canada Goose Flying with Radio Transmitter

flocks, how high and fast they fly, and what direction they are taking.

Scientists also use radio transmitters to spy on birds. That is, the scientists don't use the transmitters. The birds do. Tiny transistor radios are hung around the necks of big birds like Canada geese and wild turkeys. The radios give different beep-beep sounds as the birds walk or eat, swim or fly. Of course when the birds travel miles away

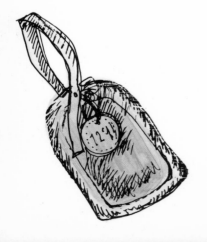

Transmitter
Carrying Case
with Tiny Radio

the scientists can no longer hear their beeps. To solve this problem, one man proposes that we launch a satellite, similar to weather satellites that are now in orbit. Circling the earth, the satellite could receive the birds' signals and send them to stations on the ground. Then we could know *exactly* what the birds were doing all the time.

The Navigators

Even a satellite couldn't answer the most puzzling question of all about the birds' fall flights. How does a robin that hatched in a nest on your street find its way to Florida? How can a whooping crane navigate from the Canadian wilds to the plains of Texas?

Just think about the problem. How do you find your way to school and home again? Probably your mother or an older child took you the first time. They showed you where to cross the street and when to turn left or right.

Now make it a little harder. Suppose that you live in Maine or North Dakota and you decide to visit your grandmother in Florida. You're not going to take a plane. You're going to walk there. At night. Without a flashlight.

But that isn't hard enough. Suppose that you don't know your grandmother's address. You know that she lives someplace in the South, and that's all. Could you find her?

And that really isn't hard enough. Because you still

wouldn't be traveling through the woods or across the ocean. You would have road signs and maps to guide you.

As you did on your first day at school, young birds often travel with their parents or follow older birds. Also, birds of all ages have excellent eyesight (perhaps three times as good as yours). They have remarkable memories too for places they have seen. They can spot familiar trees and rocks while they're flying, and remember them years afterward.

But—many young birds never travel with their parents. They fly south earlier or later, heading for a winter home that they haven't seen before. And even birds with sharp eyes can't spot a tree or rock that's a thousand miles away. How do birds know in which direction to head? How do they stay on course—or change it—during their long flight?

A scientist who was interested in bird navigation put some starlings in a big circular cage. He covered the sides of the cage so that they could see only the sun and sky. In the fall when they would ordinarily have been migrating, they fluttered around the cage and then headed southwest—the direction that they would have taken if they had been free. Sometimes the scientist turned the cage around. Sometimes he used mirrors in the cage to reflect a different part of the sky. No matter what he did, the starlings stuck to their direction. On cloudy days they perched any old place, but as soon as the sun came out, they headed southwest again.

Warblers Migrating

Another scientist tried the same sort of experiment with warblers who migrate at night. He put their cage inside a planetarium so that he could change the positions of the stars when he wanted to. The warblers had been raised indoors. They had never seen the real sky. But in the fall they guided by the stars in the planetarium and headed south.

65

After years of patient work the scientists felt sure that birds traveling in the daytime take their direction from the sun, while the night fliers get their bearings from the stars. In the fall they head southeast or southwest, staying on course by watching the sky.

It's easy to say that birds find their way by watching the sky—but it's much harder to do. A bird must not only keep track of the time, but as it flies farther and farther south it must take into account the changing position of the sun. You could do the same thing if you had a sextant, chronometer, telescope, altitude table, artificial horizon, and knew lots of geometry!

Navigators—human navigators, that is—didn't even invent some of these instruments until 250 years ago. On the most famous voyage ever made, Columbus had no sextant and his compass was undependable. He tried not to let his sailors know that he wasn't sure where he was going because, after two months at sea, they threatened mutiny if he didn't find land soon. Fortunately for all of us, it was October by then. While Columbus was arguing with his crew, a flock of birds flew by. Changing his course he followed the birds—and landed in the West Indies. If it hadn't been for the migrating birds with their built-in sextants and chronometers, we might not celebrate Columbus Day.

5. The Big Parade

When the North Pole leans away from the sun, hundreds of different kinds of creatures start to move. It's like the beginning of a parade. At the top of the world, herds of reindeer gather on the treeless tundra. Shoulder to shoulder, with antlers almost touching, they trot south to the evergreen woods. In the Rocky Mountains bands of elk clatter down the slopes to feed on grass in the valley below.

While the elk travel downhill, hordes of lady-bird beetles fly up. These are the ladybugs who are told to "fly away home." They do fly away in the fall. Thousands hide together under rocks, one on top of the other to keep warm. In some places the heaped-up beetles are several feet thick.

Salmon in the oceans head toward shore. Schools of silver-sided fish gather at the mouths of rivers. Not the warm streams of the South, but the cold, fast-moving rivers of Maine and the Northwest. As chock-full of fat as any migrating bird, they stop eating when they enter fresh water. They fight their way upstream, battling currents and leaping over rocks and waterfalls.

The rivers narrow. The fish grow thin and scrawny. Their journey ends at last hundreds of miles inland. On the gravel bottoms of mountain pools they lay eggs. Their round salmon-red eggs (called red caviar when you buy them in a grocery store) hatch the following spring.

Salmon from the Pacific Ocean die after their eggs are laid. The Atlantic salmon swim to the sea again. They will return another fall.

The most remarkable part of this remarkable journey is that the salmon are coming home. They don't lay their eggs in any pool they pass. After years of living in the ocean they swim a thousand miles and more to reach the stream where they were born.

What maps do they follow to get there? How do they recognize their homes?

Millions of salmon have been marked and tagged and studied in fish tanks. Scientists are not quite sure, but they think that when the fish are in mid-ocean they take their direction from the sun and stars, as birds do. When they swim upriver, taste and smell help to guide them. The salmon remember the special odors of the stream where they hatched and smell their way home!

Of Whales and Butterflies

Whales join the parade too. Every fall a fleet of gray whales leaves the icy Arctic Ocean for warmer waters off Mexico. Breathing through their blowholes and slapping the water with their tails, these giants of the sea follow the coast of Oregon and California as they swim south. They travel so close to shore that in the neighborhood of San Diego people line the beaches or go out in boats to whale-watch.

Not so long ago gray whales were as scarce as whooping cranes. Called "devil-fish" by old-time whalemen, they were hunted almost to extinction. Before they went the way of the passenger pigeons, the whale-hunting countries agreed not to kill them any more. Now the number of gray whales is slowly increasing again. When their calves—slippery, two-ton babies—are born in mid-winter, men from the Fish and Wildlife Service fly to Mexico to make sure that they are all right.

While some Californians are whale-watching others are waiting for butterflies. In Pacific Grove, south of San Francisco, people know that it's fall when clouds of orange and black butterflies flutter down from the sky to roost in a grove of pine trees near the coast.

Coming from as far away as Alaska, the Monarch butterflies flock to the same trees year after year. They fly through passes in the mountains and cross miles of open water to reach their winter home. Millions of butterflies cling to the branches of the pines. When they open their wings the trees seem to be covered with orange flowers.

The people of Pacific Grove are so proud of their butterfly trees that anyone who harms a Monarch there is sent to jail. But these are not the only butterfly trees in the country. Monarchs follow flyways too. The butterflies who spend summers east of the Rocky Mountains go to Texas, Louisiana, and Florida in the fall.

All over the continent on sunny days in September they drift across the fields, stopping here and there to sip nectar from goldenrod. Often they travel along the highways in twos and threes. They fly lower than the birds, beating their wings steadily as if to race the speeding cars. At night, hundreds settle down together on a tree. After the sun warms them in the morning, they move on. Day after day a long thin line of butterflies heads south.

The Monarchs' habit of roosting together at night has made it easy for scientists to study them. Each fall a professor in Canada arms himself with a huge net. He catches thousands of the butterflies while they're asleep.

Monarchs Roosting

With the help of his wife and some of his students he fastens tiny paper tags to their wings. From these gummed labels that look like Band-Aids we *know* that some Monarchs fly from Canada all the way to Mexico. We are pretty sure that the sun's rays act as their compass when they travel. That's why they rest at night and on cloudy days.

But how do these frail creatures who are long on wing and short on brain find the same trees each year? Butterflies live for only a short time. The Monarchs that arrive in Pacific Grove this fall are the grandchildren—or great-grandchildren—of those who were there last year. They are not coming home as the salmon are. They have never been in Pacific Grove before. Why don't they stop in San Francisco or fly on to Hollywood instead?

Perhaps they follow a trail that was laid down long ago. Just as men blaze a trail through the woods by marking trees with axes, so the butterflies blaze a trail by marking trees—with perfume. That's not as crazy as it sounds, because each male Monarch has a pair of scent pouches on his hind wings. When a flock of Monarchs roosts on a tree even for one night, the branches have a special strong odor. People can't always smell it, but other butterflies can.

Tracking the Bear to Its Lair

If you don't see a butterfly on the highway, maybe you'll meet a bear. A bear with a striped fur coat and sixteen stubby legs. This woolly bear is a caterpillar.

During the summer, woolly bears feed on low-growing weeds. Early in the fall they say good-by to their leafy jungle. They creep along the sidewalk. They crawl across the road. If you pick one up, it will roll into a tight ball and play dead. As soon as you put it down, it will scurry off again.

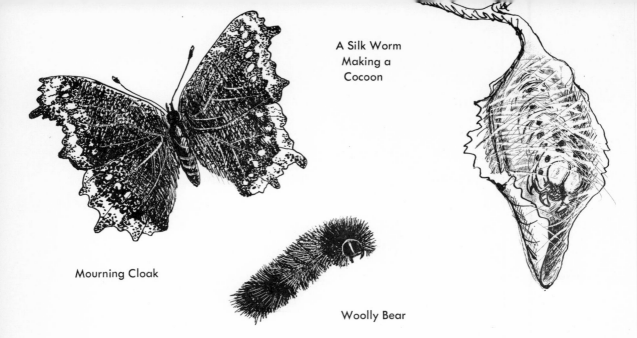

A Silk Worm
Making a
Cocoon

Mourning Cloak

Woolly Bear

Woolly bears hump along so busily that people used to speak of "hurrying like a caterpillar in the fall." They believed that the woolly bears could tell what the winter was going to be like. Some years the red-brown stripe around the caterpillars' middles is wider than in others. People thought that if the stripe was wide, the winter would be warm. If it was narrow, they expected long months of ice and snow.

Even if these caterpillars could forecast the weather, they would still have to get ready for winter because some frosty morning their favorite weed patch will be brown and dry. But how can caterpillars escape from hunger and cold? They can't fly or swim. Their legs are too short for a hike to Florida.

The woolly bears househunt instead. They look under logs and stones, and visit the far corners of porches and garages. At last they find a place that suits them. As if they were imitating their namesake, the black bear, they curl up in their dens and sleep until spring.

Hornworm and Chrysalis

6.   The Animals' Way

Most butterflies don't migrate as the Monarchs do. Most caterpillars don't wander around like the woolly bears. The Mourning Cloak butterfly takes shelter in a hollow log or woodpile; on warm days in the late winter it will fly through the woods again.

The Giant Silkworm caterpillar makes its own winter home. The silkworm stops eating and fastens itself to a leaf or branch. Hour after hour, it wraps layers of silk around its body until it is hidden away in a windproof, waterproof cocoon.

While the silkworm spins its cocoon, a fat hornworm crawls down the stem of a tomato plant. Its feeding days are over too. It tunnels under the ground. Before long it has shed its caterpillar skin and is covered from head to tail by a stiff, shiny brown wrapping.

You will never see either of these caterpillars again. During the winter as they rest in their snug sleeping bags their bodies change. When spring comes they won't be caterpillars any more. They will be handsome, broad-winged moths.

Other insects have other ways of getting ready for the change of seasons. On warm September evenings you can hear the cackling chorus of crickets and katydids. As the

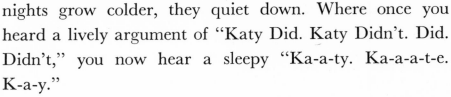

nights grow colder, they quiet down. Where once you heard a lively argument of "Katy Did. Katy Didn't. Did. Didn't," you now hear a sleepy "Ka-a-ty. Ka-a-a-t-e. K-a-y."

After a frost there is silence. The katydids are dead. So are most of the crickets. And the grasshoppers. And their ferocious-looking relative, the praying mantis.

This seems like a final sort of way to get ready, doesn't it? But—before she dies each insect mother lays eggs. The katydid's flat eggs are glued to the edge of a leaf. The field cricket and grasshopper lay theirs in the earth. The praying mantis fastens her eggs to a bush, covering them with bubbly froth which hardens when it dries.

Like the seeds on the ground, the eggs contain the beginnings of living, breathing insects. They will hatch in the spring—unless hungry birds find them.

The City-Dwellers

Anyone who goes on a picnic in early fall is sure to meet the inhabitants of the insect cities. If ants don't nibble on your sandwich, wasps will. And no wonder. The wasps are like the little old woman who lived in a shoe and had so many children that she didn't know what to do. The huge paper nest hanging from a tree was started by a single queen wasp. Now it has up to five thousand tenants. The yellow jackets—who are also wasps— have built an underground paper nest that is just as big.

The young wasps that stay in the nest are meat-eaters,

Praying Mantis

Yellow Jackets

but the grown-ups eat almost anything. They like bananas and jelly sandwiches as much as you do. In the fall when fruit is ripening, they fly to the orchard. If they find rotting apples on the ground, they get drunk on apple juice. Really drunk. They wheel around in dizzy circles and fall down.

This is the wasps' last fling. When freezing weather comes, the residents of their insect cities die. Only the queen wasps who are loaded with next year's eggs live on. They move out of their paper apartment houses and crawl through the grass looking for places to sleep. Sometimes they hide in people's homes. If you find yourself entertaining a queen this winter, don't worry. Her majesty will be too drowsy to sting.

Honey Bees

The cold sends the ants to the basement rooms of their underground cities. Honey bees stay at home too, but they heat their hives. When the last flowers have faded in the fields, the bees pile on top of each other. They move their wings and sway from side to side. The colder the day the more they exercise. Even in below-zero weather they keep warm. If they get hungry they stop and eat the honey that they have stored.

The Long Sleep

Sssh. Not an insect is stirring. The mosquitoes and flies are asleep. So are the beetles and bugs and bumblebees and the many-legged centipedes. They're hiding in cracks in the bark, or on the ground. The blanket of leaves becomes their blanket.

Sssh. The toads are asleep. With the first frosts of fall, they use their horny hind legs as shovels and dig under the ground. Turtles and frogs bury themselves in the mud at the bottom of the pond. Snakes glide under rocks. Earthworms wriggle deeper and deeper in the soil.

The fall parade is taking a brand-new direction. These creatures and a host of larger ones have found a different way to escape from winter. Like the trees in the woods, they shut up shop. They stop eating and drinking. They crawl into dens and burrows and sleep. The Indians called this "The Long Sleep." We call it *hibernation*.

Toad

Rabbit

Gray Squirrel

Raccoon

Jumping Mouse

Who hibernates? If you try to guess by looking at the pictures on this page you will probably be wrong. For the ground squirrels hibernate and the gray squirrels don't. Jumping mice sleep through the winter and deer mice don't. Although they have warm fur coats, raccoons stay in their dens while rabbits hop through the snow—and foxes chase after them.

Deer Mouse

Ground Squirrel

Among the sleepiest animals of all are the woodchucks. The fields are still green when they waddle into burrows they have dug. In the far corner of a long tunnel they tuck their noses into their tails and sink down into a deep, dreamless sleep. They never see the bare trees or the snow-covered ground above them. Winter just doesn't have a place on the woodchucks' calendar.

If your mother has trouble getting you up in the morning, tell her she ought to meet a hibernating woodchuck. No amount of shaking or shouting will wake it. People have tried rolling a woodchuck across the floor, tossing it up in the air, or dipping it into a pail of water, without breaking into its slumber.

The sleep of the woodchuck is as remarkable in its way as the travels of the terns or the homecoming of the salmon. For close to five months the machinery of its body is almost at a standstill. It scarcely breathes. Its heart slows down. Its digestion stops and its temperature drops. Its legs are stiff and cold.

Weasel in Winter Coat

Like Sleeping Beauty in the fairy tale, the woodchuck is as close to death as a living creature can be. But it doesn't die. Early in the spring it comes to life again.

Jumping mice and the striped ground squirrels of the Middle West hibernate the way woodchucks do. Their death-like sleep may last for half of the year. Chipmunks and some of their ground-squirrel relatives of the Far West sleep for shorter periods. Raccoons and bears sleep too, but so lightly that they are not considered real hibernators.

The animals can't buy snowsuits to wear outdoors. Instead, they grow their own. They molt in the fall the way birds do. Their new fur coats are longer and thicker than their summer ones. Sometimes they are a different color. Weasels who live in the North swap their old brown fur for coats of winter white. So do some of the Arctic rabbits and foxes.

Can you figure out why woodchucks don't change the color of their coats?

Many animals have year-around homes. Others build shelters or look for dens in the fall. You may have seen a squirrel running up the trunk of a tree with its mouth full of leaves. It is building a nest—a huge ball of brown leaves—near the top of the tree.

A hollow tree, a log lying on the ground, an opening under a stone wall may be a den for raccoons and foxes, skunks and opossums—but not all at the same time. These animals don't build winter homes. They take what they can find. If hollow trees are scarce, raccoons move into an old woodchuck burrow. Or they climb down the chimney of an empty summer cottage and sleep there.

Rabbits and deer stay outdoors even when it snows. Deer herd together in the fall, choosing a special place in the woods to meet in. They trample paths through the snow to find food.

82

Harvest Time

Eating is the real business of fall for the animals. They eat from morning until night, and from night until morning. They eat as if they didn't know where their next meal was coming from, and then they eat some more.

They aren't being greedy, of course. Just as football players eat steak before a big game, the animals have to fill up on nourishing food. Their big game is going to last for a long time—and they are playing for their lives.

Before they sleep, woodchucks stuff themselves on the farmer's beans and clover. When they retire to their burrows, they have thick layers of fat under their skins. Like the wax in a candle, this fat is slowly burned up during the winter.

The farmer who hunts woodchucks by day, chases raccoons at night. When the moon rises, families of raccoons head for his cornfields—and apple trees—and grape arbor. But they don't need to depend on the farmer because all of fall's harvest belongs to them. They gorge on fish and frogs, crickets and grasshoppers. They dig up yellow jackets' nests to eat the young wasps and they raid hives for bees and honey. They stand on tiptoes to catch moths that flutter around lighted windows. They patrol the highways for rabbits that have been killed by passing cars. They hunt along the flyways for injured ducks and geese.

By the time you sit down to your Thanksgiving dinner, the raccoons have finished theirs. They are padded with fat from their heads to their striped tails. A spell of freezing weather sends them to their dens. They sleep for weeks at a time, but if you knock at their door they'll wake to look at you. After a lazy yawn they'll doze off again.

Chipmunks and squirrels hardly stop to catch their breaths either. They're busy hunting for acorns, nibbling mushrooms, collecting seeds. Chipmunks don't have pockets in their coats, but they have something just as good. They carry food in pouches in their cheeks. They stuff seeds and nuts into their ballooning cheeks until they look as if they had mumps. Then they scamper off to their underground homes and unload. When they hibernate in November, they have a pile of food nearby. If they wake, they can reach out a paw for a snack.

Even the squirrels who don't hibernate store nuts and acorns. They hide them in different places, burying them, or dropping them into holes in trees. When food is scarce, they dig them up again. A scientist studied a group of flying squirrels, the smallest members of the squirrel tribe. He found that they collected more than three hundred hickory nuts on a single night in November. He discovered something else that was surprising. The squirrels have a way of marking their nuts, either with their mouths or front feet, so that they can tell which ones belong to them. The nuts that they have handled smell differently —to the squirrels, that is.

Foxes bury extra meat and fruit. Beavers keep winter supplies of twigs and bark in the pond near their lodge.

But the most interesting harvester of all is the pika, a relative of the rabbits, who lives in the Rockies.

Pikas make hay. They gather grasses and flower stems and bring them to their stone barns on the mountainside. As they add to their piles each day, they spread out the hay so that it will dry without getting moldy. Then they carry it under the rocks. Pikas are so good at hay-making that men have studied their methods in the hope of getting new ideas for farmers.

Pikas

The Signal

Woodchucks sleep and raccoons eat. Squirrels gather nuts. Pikas make hay while the sun shines. But what started the fall parade in the first place? How did the animals know that winter was on its way? What gave them the signal to get ready?

Was it a shortage of food? Not likely. In the first months of fall, there are more seeds and nuts, more insects and small animals than at any other time of the year. Besides, the hibernators fall asleep even in zoos, with plates of food by their sides.

Was it cold weather? Maybe. Frost killed the katydids and wasps and sent the frogs to the bottom of the pond. But the woodchucks were sleeping before it grew cold. The raccoons were eating hungrily then. The squirrels started to bury acorns in September.

For many of the fall paraders, shorter days are the signal. The shorter days and longer nights warn the animals to get ready. Of course they don't think about it as you do. They don't say, "Hmm. Sun's rising later every morning. Better make some winter plans."

But—while the birch leaves turn gold and the robins flock to the orchard, the animals change too. They travel to different places. Or they get hungrier and sleepier. Or they gather food and store it away. They do just what their parents and grandparents and a long line of great-grandparents have been doing for thousands of years, when the North Pole tips away from the sun.

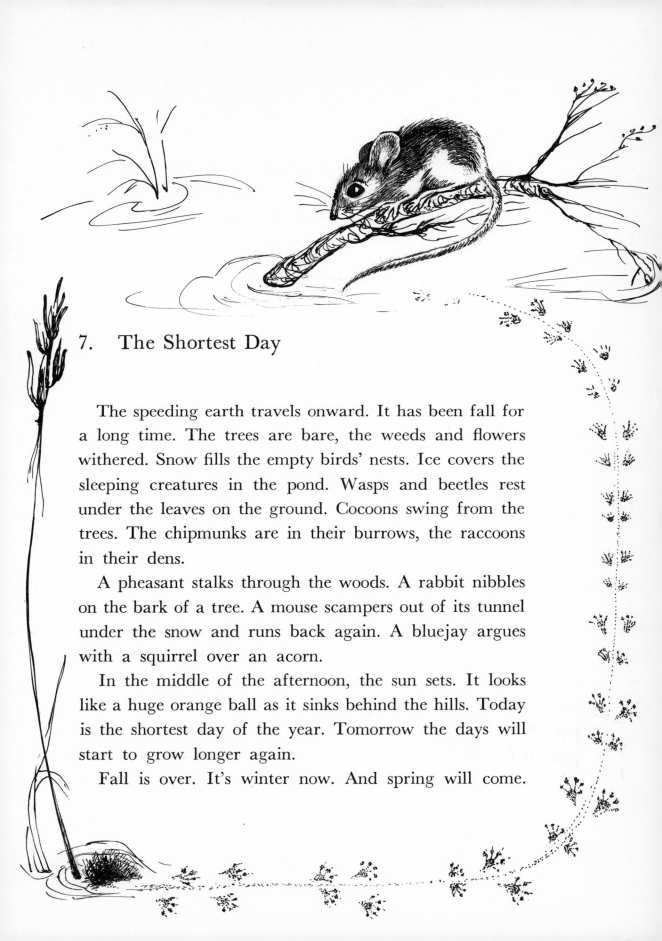

7. The Shortest Day

The speeding earth travels onward. It has been fall for a long time. The trees are bare, the weeds and flowers withered. Snow fills the empty birds' nests. Ice covers the sleeping creatures in the pond. Wasps and beetles rest under the leaves on the ground. Cocoons swing from the trees. The chipmunks are in their burrows, the raccoons in their dens.

A pheasant stalks through the woods. A rabbit nibbles on the bark of a tree. A mouse scampers out of its tunnel under the snow and runs back again. A bluejay argues with a squirrel over an acorn.

In the middle of the afternoon, the sun sets. It looks like a huge orange ball as it sinks behind the hills. Today is the shortest day of the year. Tomorrow the days will start to grow longer again.

Fall is over. It's winter now. And spring will come.

8. Things to Do in the Fall

Whether you live in the city or country, there are hundreds of interesting things to do in the fall. Here are suggestions for some of them. You will think of others.

1. A Nature Calendar

On a printed calendar or one that you make for yourself, keep a record of what you see in the fall. When do the leaves turn color? When do the milkweed seeds ripen? When do the asters bloom? When do the summer birds leave and the winter birds arrive? What was the last date on which you saw a butterfly or a yellow jacket, a turtle or a chipmunk?

If your local newspaper prints the times of sunrise and sunset and the daily temperatures, copy these on your calendar too. Next fall, look at your calendar again. Are the leaves turning color, the birds flying away, and the animals hibernating on the same dates as they did before? The longer you keep the calendar the more useful it will be. After several years you will *know* when many of the changes of fall are likely to take place. Do they seem to depend on the weather or on the length of the day?

2. A Fall Diary

Instead of a calendar you can use a notebook or diary to keep track of the plants and animals. Try to write something down every day. Many things are going on that aren't mentioned in this book. For instance, are there

Hickory

mushrooms growing from the stumps of trees? What happens to the sky at night in the fall?

3. Trees

When the leaves have fallen, look at the leaf scars on the branches of the trees. Some scars are heart-shaped, like those on the hickory. Others are oval or triangular. The big scars on the ailanthus are shaped like shields. With a magnifying glass—and a little imagination—you can see all sorts of things in leaf scars. Does the curving scar of the ash remind you of a slice of watermelon? Does the maple scar look like a mouth turned up in a smile? Can you find funny faces in other leaf scars?

Ailanthus

Notice the different colors of the branches. Some are brown, others are gray or smoky black. They smell and taste differently too. Try nibbling the tip of a sassafras twig and see if you like it.

You can make a collection of leaf scars and winter buds. Or you can arrange a bowl of tree fruit. Or you can put together the story of a single tree, starting with its seed and ending with its leaf and bud. Will there be anything missing from your story?

Ash

4. Plants

How many different kinds of seeds can you find? How many winter rosettes? You can dig up some of the winter rosettes and plant them in flower pots. If you keep them on a sunny windowsill and water them regularly some of them will grow. Will any of the seeds sprout if you plant them?

Maple

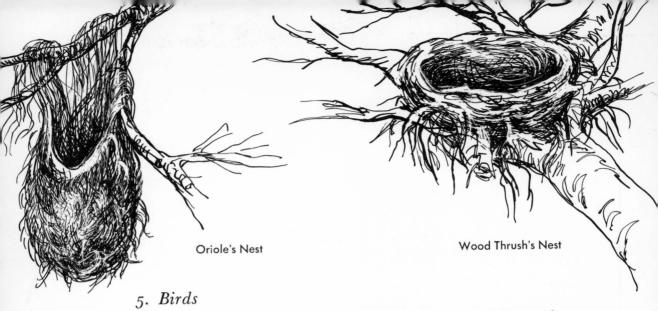

Oriole's Nest   Wood Thrush's Nest

5. *Birds*

A good time to see migrating birds is in the late afternoon. If you live near a swamp or body of water along a flyway, go there a half hour or so before sunset. Sit down quietly and wait for the flocks of birds coming in to roost.

Perhaps there are bird-banders in your town who will let you help them. Perhaps you can visit one of the wildlife refuges during the migrating season. If you can't, make the best of things by putting out food and inviting the birds to visit you.

Try several kinds of food—seeds, bread, slices of apple, peanut butter, suet (meat fat). Do different birds eat different things? Can you get a chickadee to take sunflower seeds from your hand?

Do you know what a census is? It's a count of the number of people living in one city or state. In the fall you can take a bird census, not by counting birds, but by counting their empty nests. After the leaves have fallen, you will be surprised by the number of different nests you see. How many birds nested on your street, in your school-yard, in the park?

90

Oak Gall

The birds will build new nests next spring so it's all right to collect them now. Who built the mud-lined nest in the lilac bush? Who wove the cradle that hangs from the branch of the maple tree? Any good bird guide will help you to identify the nests.

What are the nests made of? Grasses and moss, bark and twigs and mud—and newspaper and string. Orioles used to weave their stocking-like nests from horsehair. Now with so few horses around, what do they use?

6. *Insects*

Fall is the time to collect insect homes and egg-cases. Have you noticed those ping-pong balls that hang from the branches of the oak? They are *galls*. Tiny wasps laid their eggs in the oak. When the eggs hatched, the tree grew around the young wasps, forming the round balls. The wasps live in these balls during the winter. In the spring, they chew holes in the galls and fly off.

Other insects form galls in goldenrod stems, at the tips of willow branches, on hickory trees and blackberry bushes. There are more than a thousand different kinds of insect galls. How many can you find? Is the insect still inside? If not, can you figure out how it escaped?

The big paper wasp nests are safe to handle after a hard frost, but it's best to leave them outdoors for a month or two, to make sure that all of the young wasps in the paper

Goldenrod Gall

Blackberry Gall

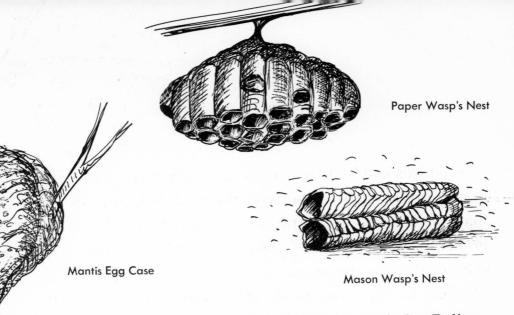

Paper Wasp's Nest

Mantis Egg Case

Mason Wasp's Nest

rooms are dead. The smaller paper nests of the Polistes wasp and the mud nests of the mason wasp can be found in garages or under porches. If you find a mason wasps' nest plastered to a wall, use a kitchen spatula to remove it. What do you see inside? Are the creatures dead or alive?

Everybody hunts eggs at Easter, but have you ever hunted for them in the fall? Look for a shiny brown bracelet on the branch of a cherry tree. It contains tent caterpillar eggs. Look for a cocoon that's decorated with twigs. Often a dozen or more hang from the same tree. Instead of housing caterpillars these cocoons are filled with bagworm eggs.

If you find the egg-case of a praying mantis, keep it in a cold place. Otherwise the eggs will hatch during the winter and you will have a hundred hungry mantises on your hands. Ordinarily they eat flies or mosquitoes, but if they can't catch these they will turn cannibal and eat each other.

While you're hunting for eggs, keep an eye out for cocoons. Most of them are on trees, but the Luna moth caterpillar spins on the ground, fastening leaves to the outside of its cocoon. Cocoons should be kept in a cool place and sprinkled with water from time to time so that they don't dry out. Scientists who study caterpillars and moths often keep their cocoons in refrigerators, but your mother may not like that.

If you collect eggs and cocoons for more than one year, write down the times that they hatch. Do they hatch in the morning or afternoon? In the first week of May or the second week of June? You'll probably find that they stick to regular schedules.

7. *Animals*

Surprisingly little is known about the small hibernators. When do turtles and frogs, snakes and salamanders go to sleep? Where do they hide? Do they hibernate together or alone? When do the chipmunks and ground squirrels disappear? Do the young retire before the grown-ups, or after? Girls and boys with sharp eyes, and notebooks and pencils, may discover things that scientists don't know.

Another puzzle that is still unsolved is how turtles, salamanders, and other creatures find their way from the woods to the pond, or from the pond to the woods in the fall. If you see a turtle crossing the road, ask it where it's going. Of course, you'll have to put your question so that the turtle can answer it. That's not as difficult as it sounds. Simply turn the turtle around, pointing it in a different direction. Will it go your way, or does it have its own plans? Turtles—and woolly bears—are so slow-moving

that if you are patient you can probably follow them on their fall wanderings. Can you think of ways to mark them, without hurting them, so that you will know them the next time you meet?

If you live in the country, put out food for animals as well as birds. Try table scraps, bread, even dog food. Squirrels will eat during the day, but when the sun sets a pink-footed opossum may come to call. If the weather isn't too cold, perhaps you will have raccoon visitors also. Will rabbits come? Or deer? What do they like to eat?

If you live in the city, visit the zoo instead. What are the hibernators doing? And what are the zoo-keepers doing about monkeys, and hippos, and other animals who normally live where it's warm? Do some of the zoo animals seem to prefer the cold weather?

8. Weather Prophets

Since the days of cavemen people have believed that animals could tell ahead of time what the winters were going to be like. The woolly bear isn't the only creature who is thought to be a weather prophet. Here are other examples:

Six weeks after the katydids start to sing, there will be a frost.

When gray squirrels' tails droop, a warm winter lies ahead. If their tails are curved over their backs, cold weather is coming.

The more nuts a chipmunk stores in his burrow, the colder it will be.

When the pikas' haystacks are big, the winter will be long.

When the Monarchs arrive in Pacific Grove earlier than usual, a cold winter lies ahead.

Even plants are supposed to be able to foretell the weather. A big crop of nuts and berries in the fall means a hard winter. The outer skins of onions are thicker when it's going to be cold. When poison ivy leaves turn red in August instead of September, button up your overcoat.

Can you collect other weather "signs"? If you talk to old people in your town, perhaps they will remember some. Don't laugh at all these beliefs. There may be a basis of truth in a few of them. Can you think of ways to *prove* whether they are true or false?

You can laugh at this, however. One fall a weather man was visiting in Alaska. He was surprised to see an Eskimo putting double-thick walls on his igloo. When he asked why, the Eskimo told him that a hard winter lay ahead.

"How do you know?" the weather man asked.

"Very simple," said the Eskimo. "I noticed that the white man has extra big piles of coal this year."

Index